THE BROKEN HEART IS THE MASTER KEY

Poems

Baruch November

Ben Yehuda Press
Teaneck, New Jersey

THE BROKEN HEART IS THE MASTER KEY © 2025 Baruch November. All rights reserved. No part of this book may be used or reproduced in any manner whatsoever without written permission except in the case of brief quotations embodied in critical articles and reviews.

Published by Ben Yehuda Press
122 Ayers Court #1B
Teaneck, NJ 07666

http://www.BenYehudaPress.com

To subscribe to our monthly book club and support independent Jewish publishing, visit https://www.patreon.com/BenYehudaPress

Jewish Poetry Project #51   http://jpoetry.us

Cover illustration by Karla Cohen, https://www.karlacohenart.com/

ISBN13 978-1-963475-70-8 pb

Library of Congress Cataloging-in-Publication Data

25 26 27 / 10 9 8 7 6 5 4 3 2 1   20250625

Contents

Introduction by by Alicia Ostriker/ vii

I

After Esav / 2
Lives upon Lives / 3
After Bracha / 4
City of No Tulips / 8
An Education / 9
The Stars Drowned Beneath Us / 10
Closer to Mars / 12
An Event for Jewish Singles / 13
The Party Continues Without Him / 14
A Match / 15
Old Flames / 16

II

The Lost Golem / 22
The Destruction of Our Temple / 25
Dance Lessons for Jews / 26
The Tiger of Detroit / 27
Self-Portrait with the Baal Shem Tov / 28
Too Little to Drink, Too Much to Remember / 32
Tourists in love / 33
To Be Wicks / 34
Victor "Young" Perez / 35
The Stocked Spring / 36
Pinstripe Gargoyle / 38
The Talmud's Fool / 39
Another Soul in Passage / 40

III

The Pop-Up Rave of Jerusalem / 46
Throughout the 7th Night / 47

A Gift in the Shallows of the Sea / 48
Another Return / 49
The Tethered Life / 50
For a Few Holy Sparks / 52
You are Witness / 53
Bitter Departures / 54
The Sharp Point of the Heart / 56
The Chronicles of Never / 60
The Hour of Regret / 61
The End is the Beginning is the End…. / 63
The Loudest Language / 70

Acknowledgments and Profound Thanks: / 72
About the Author / 73

Introduction
by Alicia Ostriker

At the very start of this semi-autobiographical volume we find the place of the split. "Why are you not married" is the opening line of the opening poem. Threaded through the book, in mostly short-line poems whose language is at once plain in phrasing and lyrical in feeling, is the answer to that question: one failed romance or crush after another, done in tones of nostalgia and regret. And the poet is always looking for a woman, while "She's always revving/her silver convertible,/ roof down, racing/ away from me."

The other half of the split centers on kin and on the material world of flesh, food, clothing, dancing, towns and cities, shuls and cafes, evocatively inhabited by types like the "old butcher confessing/ that he doesn't need the messiah," he'd rather hear his long-dead father sing the blessings. Two roads, like Frost's, one romantic and spiritual, one earthy and objective? Yes. But unlike Frost, November chooses both. Great grandma Bracha, seamstress whose name means blessing, sews "a yellow dress, /like an overturned buttercup /weaved with moonlight." And all his worlds are straddled by the Baal Shem Tov, with a Jewishness layered by Yiddishkeit and mysticism.

Many Jewish poets steer away from G-d. Not November, for whom "wherever you go,/ every particle is just/ the presence/of G-d." And standing alone is the sentence fragment questioning, "How to make G-d happy/ a man alone, without children." I inhaled when I read that bit, for "a man alone, without children" is the poet; and is also G-d. Make what you will of it. My own conclusion is that the poet, and the poet's G-d, are lonely for the Shekhinah. Perhaps she will come out of hiding in November's next book. Perhaps she is present. semi-recognizable, in all those disappearing women?

Alicia Ostriker is author of The Holy and Broken Bliss *and former poet laureate of New York State.*

I

After Esav

Why are you not married?
the rabbis of my early days
demand of me
in my raging dreams.
Like the gatherers of old,
I have scavenged
the world for answers,
reassured myself
the problem is not
in the plainness
of my reflection
or the burning color
of my hair— the color of
that ancient hunter,
that great sinner
whose body was lust-driven,
and who bit his brother's neck
when they embraced,
only to find it made of marble
for that instant
and come away
as hungry as ever.

Lives upon Lives

Contractors affix buildings on top
of buildings in Jerusalem.
Occupants below must clear out
for all the years it takes
to finish adding
to sandstone structures.

I have lived lives upon lives.
I want to go back
to when I was certain—it was my twenties.
I dismissed many great women.
Someone greater was always coming along.

I have been an inept architect.
I built for one who does not live
with the truth of others.
I built for starlight,
not shelter.

I built for ghosts
of those never born.
I built a hollow home
for howling winds.

I built a demise
in waiting
and thought it
a masterpiece
towering over
the settled lives
of others.

After Bracha

My mother reminds me
I am named after
her grandma Bracha
who brought her sweet
poppy seed pastries.

Bracha mastered the parting
of childhood darkness—
making excellent stuffed
cabbage and strudel:
delicacies for the delicate heart.

      ***

Until dying, her husband, Yishiya,
held a great distaste for work
but peddled junk on the streets of Erie
in a horse-drawn wagon
instead of a truck— a mark
of shame on his family burning
like a streak left from a whip.

      ***

Bracha is the Hebrew word
for blessing. For its bearer,
a lot to live up to.

A version of the word begins
the blessing before a Jew eats,
even if the food is cold gruel,

Even if the food prods memory:
a recipe from shtetls of
impaled mothers, children, scribes.

      ***

Bracha, a master seamstress,
made a yellow dress,
like an overturned buttercup
weaved with moonlight,
for my grandmother—an expert
complainer all her life,
who managed to degrade
the glowing outfit, calling it
old country fashion.

***

We read numerous
blessings in thanks:

A blessing for just being able
to arise in early pink-blue light.

A blessing for when lightning veins
a cloud or strikes the oak into flames.

A blessing for when the earth quakes:
sacred pictures of your family—
all you have left of them—
launching from the walls
into lethal puzzles of glass.

A blessing for the first time
the ocean spreads before you,
multitudes filling azure depths,
sunlight igniting tips of waves.

A blessing for the rare
beautiful creations:
the matriarchs Rachel and Sarah,
Queen Sheba of Ethiopia,
Queen Esther of Persia,
Tamar, daughter of David,

Yael, killer of Sisera,
Avishag, who pressed
her young body against
David in his dying days
just to keep him warm.

      ***

In '54, her husband died.
Bracha moved in with her
daughter's family in Pittsburgh.
She took care of everybody—
even the dogs, feeding them
cow brains they loved.

G-d stole much of her
family in pogroms—
still she kept kosher,
refusing to eat meat out.

This was the one
thing she carried
from a shtetl
called Pliskov.

      ***

Bracha drank hot water
with cherry jam for dessert,
turning the liquid to dark rubies—
warm sweetness erasing
memory for an instant.

      ***

Bracha also means to draw down.
When we bless our challah,
our livelihood, or the blowing

of the shofar, we draw G-d
to this world, says the Zohar,
like children calling to parents
out of the darkness.

    ***

Bracha later married a Jersey man
named Abe, who made a big deal
of promising her a wonderful life—

But hoarded every cent he had,
while she spoiled him with
kugels and apple pastries.

Abe died and left Bracha
nothing but the spite of
a single dollar in his will.

    ***

Sholom Shachna, Bracha's father,
was the shtetl's teacher.
He ensured Bracha read
and wrote Yiddish.

All her life, she loved
to correspond
with friends,
kept a notebook,
pale blue lines—
the normal color
of sky when clear
and heavy flames
do not whip
and wave out
of thatched roofs.

The Broken Heart is the Master Key

City of No Tulips

At the mouth of the river
Amster stood the great city
of museums and tulips.

The rain slanted into dusk.
Bicycles threw puddles
into chaos. Green canals
churned with old sorrows.

I didn't see any tulips.
Either they were out
of season or I was.

An Education

Sometimes you still have to
remind yourself you won't be

That teenager again
in a Hebrew Day School,

Who painfully shied from the eye doctor's daughter
and was too serious

About reading Hawthorne and listening to Leonard Cohen
sing *from the other side of sorrow and despair,*

Who became furious playing basketball
on the school's makeshift court:

Sometimes when you shot, the ball did not
complete its arc, hitting the too low

Ceiling of possibilities
with the rasping sound

Of a crude machine rejecting
everything it's fed.

You began to know then
what life is like—

Exactly what
it should
not be.

The Stars Drowned Beneath Us

My grandpa liked to joke
that his only mistake
was in ever thinking
he could make one.

I've never had that kind
of nerve, but he could bash
a tiger shark dull with it,
then wrestle away all
of life's shadows, storm clouds,
roiling gray tides—while
eating warm corned beef
on pumpernickel
out of his left hand.

Maybe all this came from times
he calmed his mother when
she was struck by memory
of the pogroms:
her parents had gagged her
in fear she would cry out
over the cries outside
their hiding place.

Maybe it started when his father,
the butcher, had heart trouble,
and my grandpa dropped out
of high school to take over.

Once a lady asked him
if the ground meat was fresh
again and again and again
until he took a handful of it—
pressed it against her face.

Maybe it was the kind of certainty
a young man gets to keep
for killing Nazis with skill
or serving as the pilot who flew
Marlene Dietrich wherever
she needed to go.
(He said she was beautiful
like no one else, walking
that pale lit airfield.)

Ages later, on his boat,
with my brother and me,
he could still use that easy
confidence to return us
from passage over
mad Atlantic waves
cresting so high,
the brightest of stars
hissed out
as they drowned
beneath us.

Closer to Mars

Before I could master Pilates,
the city embraced goat yoga.
Robots improvised autofiction,
publishing it under the names
of dead engineers. The authorities
believed in the immortality
of plastic bags but not in G-d.

An Event for Jewish Singles

Other people know how
to enjoy themselves.
I am a miserable guest,
especially at these parties
where spinning asteroids
collide or veer off
on their own: you know, lonely

Strangers attempting to meet
over terrible music—
but it turns into a couple hours
where I stare at my phone,
the cedar wood ceiling,
or pray against my self-
destruction.

Or I rewind the night
because I can in a poem
and stay home, listen
to the glowing horn
of Miles Davis, read
a mystical tract
about how much soul
actually needs body
and body needs soul.

I learn how G-d needs
even me, for nothing
could have been created
for the sake of nothing.

The Party Continues Without Him

Nietzsche proclaimed,
He who has let go
of G-d clings all
the more strongly
to the belief
in morality
like the bald man
overboard clings
to the cold buoy,
knowing that having fallen
after dusk, the party
will continue
long into his
desperate night
of a billion
careless stars.

A Match

> *How can anyone have you and lose you*
> *and not lose their mind too.*
> *—St. Vincent*

Freud, of course, would've told me
never to love a girl who shared
a first name with my mother.

But she was from Havana
and would floor her silver BMW
with me beside her
into the darkness of Jersey City.

I tried hard to make it last—
so it ended.
She made sure a few months later
to tell me *it was never love,*
but I knew what I knew.

Curious, I wrote to her years later,
knowing she had married,
asking her if
she had children yet.

She didn't write back,
then said *no,*
and I told her *how very
surprised I was*—

To which there was no answer,
as my sadness
had found its match
in my cruelty.

Old Flames

1

All my elementary years I loved fire.
I liked the little fireworks that looked
like dynamite sticks.
I took one to school, put it in a blood-
red plum to silence the sound,
lit the fuse....

Rabbis never seen before
came running as if they had
been created from nothing
but the sound itself.

2

*The difference between a good life
and a bad life is how well you walk
through the fire*, said Carl Jung.

3

Called a city,
Scranton is almost one.
A local arsonist captured
this insecurity, never
targeting tall buildings
or the homes of the rich—
only ramshackle tool sheds
behind lower class
houses, burning them up
in hapless blazes.

4

Jung must have dreamt
of Abraham thrown

in the immense furnace
by King Nimrod of Babylon.

Abraham walked inside
for three days without
even a blister.

Only the heavy rope
that bound him
burned away.

5

Scranton once had
a heart of coal.
Nothing can glow
that bright now.

6

Nimrod was a trapper of men
and animals. When he roasted
a gazelle over the flames,
did he see himself rising

over everyone
in the distortions
of heat and ash?

Did flames or stars tell
him to worship idols
and condemn those
who did not?

He must have known
from how well he snared all
living things that he would
someday be king.

7

Luther Perkins, guitarist
on Johnny Cash's *Ring of Fire*,
burned away in a bed
of rising flames,
the last of his cigarette
falling from his lips
as he began to dream.

8

I adored the sulfur smell
smoke bombs gave off
in colored curls rising up
after their fuses shot out
little sparks like my own
personal lightning.

9

Abraham touched the name of G-d
that is higher than nature,
so flames couldn't touch him.

10

Somewhere above,
an orchestra of fire plays,
incinerating the edge
of a galaxy, and a sun
explodes to end
some old solar system.
A long hiss….

The worlds are gone—
like that bronze-haired woman
I lacked the nerve

to approach that May night
in the Bowery
when I turned to order
a double shot of bourbon.

11

King Nimrod's stargazers
warned him of Abraham,
and the constellations
must have already moaned
in defeat. Their lights
dulled like the eyes
of an old merchant
with no way home.

12

Who by fire?
we wonder every
Rosh Hoshana
in our prayers.

In July of '41,
it was the Jewish
women and children
of Riga sealed inside
The Great Choral Shul.

13

Lester Perkins' play
on the Fender Esquire,
the Jazzmaster,
the Jaguar Guitar
gave Johnny Cash
his signature driving sound.

The home that burned around
Lester had been just built.
He made it alive
to the hospital
but no further.

14

You might have never
heard of that old
massacre on Gogol Street;

Listen to any of Riga's
old stone roads.
You will hear
a blaring silence—
a refrain of shame.

15

My love of fire ended
before high school.

A body worthy of not burning
held my soul in this world

The way sheet music
keeps its song.

II

The Lost Golem

1

Her thesis ties *The Scarlet Letter*
to the works of early Kabbalists.
Her slender body slips
into hidden worlds.

Parts of her ankles and knees
dimple when she bends,
consuming light
in their creases.

When offended,
tiny silver sparks flash
from the inner corners
of her eyes,

And when she scribbles
a note or looks for her keys,
her fingers flutter
like startled thrushes
so bright their contours
merge with all
they might touch.

2

She recalls the starlit river
of your former lives—
says you met there before
the old country was old.

Was it Hungary or Poland?
What about Prague?
Wherever it was,
the people saw G-d

as eternal scaffolding
that enclosed everything.

3

She bats her long eyelashes,
almost lets you
kiss her, almost allows you
a precise reading
of the Kabbalistic text
wrinkled into her dark
red lips— which always
defies translation.

But it doesn't matter:
she closes that book
before you bring its words
to your mouth,

Claims with certainty
you are the past;
there is a younger man
waiting for her—
how could you not
have known?

4

Burning, you withdraw,
and after you cool,
you become a golem,
wandering a wasteland
of others— trying anything
just to stifle the starving
that is just you
looking for another.

5

Like a beam of light,
loneliness seems infinite:

Your intended's lineage
must have severed long before
she could even exist—
her ancestors rounded up
at Babi Yar or some place
no longer on a map,

Which, if you found it now,
would not contain one
Jewish headstone
or anything else to hint
at whose name
might have perched
on the slender tree
of family history
next to yours.

The Destruction of Our Temple

If we sleep together, the Cuban Jew said,
it means I love you.
3 days later, she said nothing more.

If I say nothing to you, it is over,
she did not say,
so I called and called.

At his wedding, Daniel asked,
What is wrong with you?
I said nothing—tried hard
to look happy dancing
in the ring of Chassidic men.

I clapped when they broke
    the glass hastily hidden
    under the white cloth.
    Shards flew at everyone.
But, in love, there is no one
to yell *Watch out*
and no one would listen
if someone did.

Dance Lessons for Jews

Something about Chassidim
dancing makes Jews
feel more like Jews—

Or like rejecting everything
mystical out of old fears,
leaving the synagogue
though it's cold out
now for Jews.

Return is always possible
to the circles of deep believers
who do not relate dance
to the delicate art of dark swans.

One Talmudic master
was so renowned for wildly
dancing at weddings— swinging
twigs of myrtle above his head—
that others said he'd degraded
the reputation of scholars.

They had missed the point—
which was to touch
the joy of belief
beyond understanding.

The Tiger of Detroit

Every one of his home runs
in 1938 was hit off of Hitler.
Rage transformed
into urgency
in the batter's box.

He wanted so much to amaze those
who called him *Christ-killer,
sheenie, kike, pant-presser.*
They say only Jackie Robinson
had it worse.

When he did not play on Yom Kippur,
he electrified the fasting
congregation: tall shul doors
opened to reveal
the tiger slipping through.

The rabbi pounded his pulpit for silence.
Women swiveled their necks,
children stood on their chairs
to catch a glimpse of Greenberg–

A man who never played cards,
knowing his teammates
would holler if a Jew
threw down a full house,
a royal flush—
taking all their earnings
home to buy his wife
a necklace bright
as the closest
strand of stars.

Self-Portrait with the Baal Shem Tov

Let me fall if I must fall.
The one I will become
will catch me,
said the Baal Shem Tov.

You keep falling but learn
nothing new. You land
in cold currents of regret,
sending shocks to your soul,
but it does not awaken.

      ***

The Baal Shem Tov died
on a sacred holiday.
His followers forbidden
to bury him,
he buried himself:

Another selfless act
in a life of piety, while
you push yourself just
to pray in the morning—

Not stare at snow tumbling
down dark grey
Washington Heights sky—

And ask G-d to match you
with a woman whose *lamp*
does not go out at night.

      ***

If you lived in the time
of the Baal Shem Tov— wielder

of G-d's hidden names—
you'd take a one-horse wagon
over Carpathian foothills,
Ukraine's hard, snowy roads,
hoping he would bless you
with a family and the secrets
of the holy curves on Hebrew
letters to teach your children.

 ***

When the Baal Shem Tov closed his eyes
in the mikvah, he could see
the unity of all worlds.

You can hardly plan a trip
to Brooklyn for volumes
on the Torah's soul,
no matter
  how clearly
subway lines spread out
on the screen.

 ***

*The world is full
of wonders and miracles,*
said the Baal Shem Tov,
*but man takes his
little hand, covers
his eyes, and sees
nothing.*

 ***

Five dates with the slender
heart doctor from Flatbush
with improbable green eyes
and you're bored.

The Broken Heart is the Master Key

The matchmaker tells you
not to screw this one up;
this girl likes you.

You lack the imagination
needed to see her softly
inhabiting your future.

Only looking back
can you see her
promise— a glimpse
at the sun falling
into the sea over
your shoulder.

    ***

You want to believe down
the winding staircase,
up the twisting lane,
with the same power it took
to divide the Red Sea,
you will be united
with a woman
with a silver cup
of wine so sweet
you'll almost forget
all the long years
of longing.

    ***

When you close your eyes,
you wonder where
that heart doctor is now;
it's too late.

You try to remember
her name—hidden
among the names of others
who deserved better.

    ***

The Baal Shem Tov taught that
everyone travels 42 journeys
in life, some fraught
with neglected chances,
lonely bedrooms.

Yet there is no place
for hopelessness:
Wherever you have been,
wherever you will go,
every particle is just
the presence
of G-d.

Too Little to Drink, Too Much to Remember

Caesarea— so many years ago.
Scarlet flowers flooded the fields.
So many heavy promises.
You were my first—
I was too weak to say no more.
Pink setting sun throbbed
in windows. I opened
your white robe like a box
from the bakery.
I didn't look to your eyes
until night fell.
We stayed at a secular kibbutz
where everyone believed
we were husband and wife.
Near the entrance,
on a short column,
there was a bust—
a sour face
that had too little
to drink, too much
to remember.

Tourists in love

      are not in love with each other—
but with the moment.
It was unlucky then he only met her
on his visit to Tzfat.
Even the holiness
of the land could not bind.

Atop the high city,
they took in lush miles
of the Upper Galilee.
The moment was nothing

compared to the knowledge that
Kabbalists hid under the city's
cemetery and purifying secrets swirled
in the cold spring of the Ari's mikvah.

He lowered his lips to hers.
They were accepted
since they needed only be
tasted that one night,
when no star fell,
and the slivered moon,
behind dense clouds,
bore no witness.

To Be Wicks

I think because the Jews are weak
the Holocaust happened, said the husky Sicilian
student wearing the blue Giants jersey in the front row.
No one there corrected him—
not the visiting Jewish professor
who was busy pushing his gold-wire glasses
to the bridge of his nose.
We were weak in that immense classroom.

But after ages of being trampled,
buried in shallow pits,
racked in the Inquisition,
experimented upon by the master race,
still we build
our schools and shuls everywhere,
learn our mystical texts
telling us that only our bodies serve
as wicks for the flames of G-dliness,
and when we burn,
we burn, we burn, we burn,
we do not burn out.

Victor "Young" Perez

The Jewish flyweight from Tunisia—
who modeled himself after the Battling Siki,
a boxer from Senegal—
should have died early in the ring,

Or with a beautiful actress
in a car accident
under torrential rain
on the way to Monaco,

Or of a brain hemorrhage
late in life
deep in his sleep.

"Young" Perez was shot
among birch tree shadows
on the death march

From the labor camp
in Monowitz, where he
made synthetic rubber—

His long right arm stretched
to give a slice of bread
to another Jew.

The Stocked Spring

In the northern kibbutz
of the Galilee region,
all I learned was of longing,
a dirty dish-conveyer belt,
fields of rusted irrigation,
conformity of chicken coops,
how hard, sallow dates smelled
of love crushed under foot.

Near the entrance: a spring
stocked with rare fish.
Their odd colors streaked
as we lunged into cool water.

The unusually beautiful
girl from Manchester
covered in freckles,
hair red like mine, eyes pale
blue— nothing like mine—

Turned to me
on our first meeting,
treading those pure waters,
and smiled: *Who's this?*

My throat wouldn't
answer—full of sand
from years of wandering
the wilderness and never
finding anyone like her.

And that history told me,
you will never have her—
so I continue
in fields of exile,
a great believer

love only ripens
for others.

Pinstripe Gargoyle

Yogi's worst day was picking out
bloated bodies from the ocean
after D-Day. When he came home,

Everyone said he didn't look
like a Yankee golden boy.
Newspapers called him *gargoyle*.

From the road, he'd write
his wife: *I love you, I love you,
I love you. I went three
for four today.*

He'd swing at everything.
Thick monster wrists made him
fast enough to hit wild pitches—
never striking out.

People made fun of his face
to his face. But Yogi said,
*Who cares about your face
you don't hit with it?*

The Talmud's Fool

The Talmud classifies a fool
as one who loses
everything you give him.
I lost the Cuban Jew
a few days after
she claimed she loved me,
sitting bare-legged
on my wide windowsill—
her body backlit
by shafts
of morning light.
No explanation given.
No call returned.

Don't we all turn
into fools, though,
sooner or later,
losing everything
since we take
nothing with us
to the hereafter?

Another Soul in Passage

1

I should have known
better than to pursue
a 27-year-old Jew
from Martinique,
with a long fine face.

Compared to her smooth skin,
I felt as old as a rock-covered well
in the Negev Desert.

2

After our third date,
she posted a video
of herself dancing
too close to her
personal trainer.

A slender pink dress—
bright as a pulsar—
framed her
like a masterpiece.

A necklace dangled
down her dark skin
with stones cut
from the North Star.

3

Waiting outside her
East Side building,
I convinced myself
nothing was better

than watching
the heavy rain fall
through lamplight.

When she finally came down,
her great black eyes
were the color
of lonely darkness
crushed down
into ashtrays.

4

I don't remember ever kissing you,
she said—and I knew why
Billie Holiday sang
*Autumn in New York is often
mingled with pain.*

Instead of walking away,
I repeated the words of the Zohar:
*a king without a queen is neither
a king, nor great.*

5

If only Francesa Sarah of Tzfat,
the great Kabbalist, would deem
my dreams important enough
to visit from the afterlife
to reveal the secret behind
why I have never married.

But I am unworthy of
visits in my snoring sleep—
I go days without prayer
like a cellist strumming away
without sheet music.

6

Walking Lexington without her,
I watched a half-moon conceal
itself over the dense city—
like mysteries of the Torah
we don't deserve to understand.

7

She soon mastered kissing me
without kissing me:

Her dry lips against mine—
but sealed like a vault

Of Kabbalistic scrolls
inscribed with secrets of how to see

If the soul of another matches yours
or is just here in brief passage

To do its one intended deed
and return to the world of light.

8

I gave her pale purple flowers
for her birthday.

She adored their scent, held them
to the cashmere darkness

Of her dress. Three heavily
layered babushkas
in the next booth— or the next
world already—prepared

to celebrate, asking,
Are you engaged?

No, no, she was quick to say—
and arms of black smoke reached
out from the open kitchen.

III

The Pop-Up Rave of Jerusalem

August burns white hot.
The street— whose name
means the son of Judah—slopes
downward to Yaffo Street,
but the dancers don't mind.

They dance till inseparable,
till they don't feel the heat
and become the heat,
till their skin turns
a greater shade of tan,
till they believe they're not
of this lower world.

Israelis and tourists
in taut clothing
spin— shekels flying
from their pockets
to the street's black tiles.

"What the hell is this?"
many who pass the gate ask
the bouncers in envy,

But it is too late— no room
behind the high fence
where sweat is exchanged
like a sweet commodity

And bodies grind away
at their G-dly souls.

Throughout the 7th Night

In Jerusalem, those who believe themselves
righteous holler *shabbos*,
                             shabbos,
                                            shabbos
at sleek cars driven through
narrow streets.

This rift between Jews once led
the world's holy capital to crumble
in the days of prophecy.

All of us should be sharing wine,
braided bread, on the 7th night,
no matter how we arrive
or how we leave—

But not before saying,
L'chaim,
        l'chaim,
                l'chaim,
                        louder
than thunderclaps above
the Jordan River,

As the world to come
slips over this one.

The Broken Heart is the Master Key

A Gift in the Shallows of the Sea

Treading clear water in late July,
my father thanks me for pushing him to go
to the cool Mediterranean—
out of a heatwave so strong
it distorts both the present
and the future.

There are jellyfish warnings,
but we see only one
pale poisonous body
drifting away, mid-wave.

One night, on Riis Beach,
years ago, I suddenly
proposed to your mother
in the moonlight,
my father tells me
for the first time;

The tide drifting distance
between us, the shared
fact drawing us close.

His story, a gift
in the shallows
of the sea as waves
gleam in lines
scrawled by
the sun.

Another Return

The guest speaker's proclaiming
a dead rabbi the messiah
drove the tiny shul into seething debate
as the congregants drank cold,
burning fingers of French vodka,
chewed on tight, spiraled pastries,
ringed with hard chocolate
until the roaring
                dispute was blunted
by an old butcher confessing
that he wanted the messiah—
but he'd be happy hearing his
long-gone tuneless father sing
the blessings again over terribly
sweet wine, carve a large challah
to exact pieces for six siblings,
and stare through
the steam curling off
lentil soup that dulls
the severe edges
of this world
once more.

The Tethered Life

Short and silver-haired, the survivor
of the Kindertransport
says, *Vienna was beautiful—
the people were not.*

Edith recalls the journey
but doesn't speak of
the parents dissolving
eternally behind the train
into the distance.

She prefers wise sayings
to poetry— reminds us,
a stitch in time saves nine,
rubbing arthritic hands carefully together.
She was married long ago,
no children.

I've lived long enough, she says.
Guess my age.
April clouds obscure sunlight.
Shadow seizes the studio apartment.
Edith disdains lamplight.

99 she reveals but hopes to witness
the coronation of the new king,
even if he doesn't seem royal.
Edith once lived in England,
still has one foot
over the ocean—another
in her last chapter.

She was an architect
concerned with transformation
of hospitals to colleges, libraries
to morgues, seminaries to prisons....

A man dangles in
a canary-yellow harness off
scaffolding across the way.
A sable mustache drapes over
his mouth, as he replaces
warped gray shingles
with deep brown ones—

How much that tethered life
must be worth high above
the great variety
of sorrow below.

For a Few Holy Sparks

Says the Talmud,
Good to heaven and good to man
are the righteous.

I can be good to heaven,
reminding myself G-d directs
all universes
with love, strength, and beauty,
as the Kabbalists say.

But there is an old man who steals
my newspaper from the stoop,
there are smug people who wear happiness
as a uniform of high rank,
there was a slim redhead who never showed
as I waited on Columbus and 96th....

I would trade all
these bitter flavors,
my few holy sparks,
for a bit of heavy
forgetting, a long kiss
up the side
of my neck before
the pink clouds
of dawn.

You are Witness

How long ago was it
the Baal Shem Tov shocked
his followers by leaving in the middle
of Shabbos prayers
for hushed morning light
to follow a great black bear
to the house of a Christian judge?

Everyone watched as the bear lifted
the judge's dining room table
and dug up a baby's body
that was meant to be used as a blood libel.
The Baal Shem Tov yelled out,
You are witness,

and still,
we are witness even if we argue
this is America,
even if Yiddish is dead
or dying, even if
our ancestors
threw their tefillin
into the depths
of the East River
to celebrate release
from a G-d who
loved them—
and still loves
them beyond
measure.

Bitter Departures

The tasting at Tishbi Winery serves
French chocolate with red wines.
The chocolate opens up
taste buds to the wines
and the wines open up
heavy secrets inside.

Outside, a wide tree of
golden flowers shifts
branches in hot winds.
As if survival experts,
blossoms seem to nod,
acknowledging escape
to the vineyard's shade
would save no one.

  ***

Down the road, at the center
of Zikhron Ya'akov, a town
Baron Rothschild built,
remain the homes
of the Aronsohns —
a family of master spies
in World War I.

  ***

Sara Aronsohn—captured, tortured—
managed to shoot her own throat,
preventing her from giving up
the others.

That scarlet bloom of plasma killed
her four days later.

***

Avsholom, Sarah's brother-in-law, tried
to get a message across the Sinai
only to be caught, shot, buried, then found
years later entangled in roots of a tree.

It is said the tree arose
from a date in his pocket,
a new life from the dead—
sweet clusters shaking out
of a bitter departure.

***

Our short, talkative tour guide
was an immigrant living
by the waters of the Galilee.
Having lost his wife
a month earlier, he knew
the ways of sorrow,
the directions of loss—
a perfect guide
for the land.

The Sharp Point of the Heart

1

The town of Beit Shean lies at the juncture
of the Harrod and Jordan Valley—
like the sharp point of the heart.

Those who dwell there claim it
to be the hottest place
lived in year-round.
I won't visit again.

Flashbacks of how you
would run across the square
in oversized blue work clothes
would crush me.

Or worse, I would remember
the evening our group toured
Ein Gedi: I found you
alone, drifting behind
in the warm waters,
your long t-shirt glistening
over your body
in the pink sun....

2

Our leader, a plump American:
Everything he'd plan fell apart—
made with quicksand.
*It doesn't matter
if the program sucks,*
he'd say, *as long as
it's run by nice people.*

He did achieve
a manicured mustache,
but at the V-neck
of his shirt mad jungles
of russet hair thrived.

3

Your parents visited from
London. You ignored them;
I had to answer your
father's business chatter,
your mother's defeated silence—

And outside that Haifa café,
your chestnut hair
bound back, why did
you abruptly demand
I kiss your pale red
mouth in front of them?

4

A Swedish Jew knew everything—
Socrates and Freud spoken
in Swedish to countrymen.

In boredom, he shaved his
brown hair, enflaming
the kibbutz's Holocaust
survivors. The committee
forced him into a navy-
blue fishing hat.

5

A Liverpool girl: ripe cheeks,
hair evading description—

hazelnut, dappled blond, sometimes
all blond— somehow always sunlit.

As if to compete,
her slender friend's hair burned red
like beautiful sorrow.

Both could make a man nervous,
ask all about him—only to ignite
dreams— and move on.

But you would sneak up on me,
smelling of the esrog grove,
kiss my lower
neck, as stars flared out,
the edges of darkness rushing
outward to escape
some sad fate.

6

Slanted morning light turned
your hazel eyes golden
like the rounded bodies of pocket watches.

I can see your tall, clumsy body skip
across the autumn path to tell me
that the Swede was jogging
around the kibbutz in nothing
but the fishing hat.

7

I remember your hoarse laughter
when I threw dates
at the touchy kibbutzniks.

Like life, those yellow fruits were harder
than imagined, but would soften
within weeks, just as you did.

Daylight grew tender pink.
My hand ran up your back.
Why did you finally give
into my obvious wanting?
Why was your Ashkenazi
body always tan even
in a season overcast?

We fit in a slender bed together.
Your infinite curls poured off
the side. The scent of unripe
pomegranates crawled
under the indigo drapes.

8

You always hungered for
anything to laugh at;
you'd laugh hard
if you read this now,
decades later, seeing me
living in the long ago.

I deserve that mockery
for promising you
Next year, next year—afraid
of saying, *This is the end*,
before I climbed the marble
stairs to my flight.

The Chronicles of Never

I've never followed the steps
of a scorpion into the heat
of the Jordan Valley.

Nor have I sung sweetly enough
to ever lead davening and call
down the Shechinah.

On my shelf sits a roll of film
of Eilat I have never developed.
Each year, it loses vibrancy
until one day
it will become a darkness

Instead of a luminant city
by the Red Sea that draws
tourists in awful
neon T-shirts.

I have never fully understood
Yehuda Amichai's thing
for tall flight attendants— I am still
waiting for my coffee.
There are lips

My fingers should have
traced like braille,
nights that should have been
of a tenderness
not to mention,

And I've never gathered ghost orchids
for a fine woman— petals
fragile but pale
as the flash of light
that always comes
with a knockout.

The Hour of Regret

In new hats, Jewish tourists wander
long Manhattan blocks—
July heat biting down on them.
Floors shake with trains below.
Traffic howls out. Humidity
will not surrender.
Night can't come soon enough.

Tables bloom outside kosher cafes.
Cold white wine glows with a light
not its own.
The tourists look for minyans
offering prayer before nightfall.

Bookstores remain cool, inviting.
Department stores demand entrance,
though their silver mannequins only
dance when no one looks.

The city's mottled birds arise
from walking shadows—
iridescent wings always
fighting gravity
when least expected.

A former synagogue holds a theater.
When it's empty, countless versions
of Othello perfect the light on
their tears for the wistful ghosts
of Desdemona wandering the halls
till the first act begins again.

Mice choke on the fallen remains
of personal histories.
The hour of regret finds you again.
How to make G-d happy
a man alone, without children.

And a fragment of a dream flashes:
the wife you've never had
rushes down a star-shattered
hallway—only to struggle
at the other end
to open the door to life.

The End is the Beginning is the End....

Old and young from the start,
you'd have known me
by my brooding & curiosity.
I hid behind my mother
when I entered kindergarten.

The teacher's last name was Rope;
from the early days of schooling,
I felt tied down.

      ***

Time tilts backwards
till it moves forward:
*The end wedged
in the beginning,
the beginning wedged
in the end*, The Book of
Formation tells us.

This is not a time travel story.
This is how the mystics tell time.
To refute it, call upon
the theories of physics,
an army of guesses
arrayed to spoil
the beautiful logic of belief
we would see
if we dreamed awake
like Chassidim
studying the soul
of the Torah.

      ***

It is said that time, like love,
is a construct or illusion—

Some loves end
before they begin
at first kiss,
silent road,
fading darkness—

Morning sweeping up
the horizon like truth
or lie gone wild
in a gossiping crowd
as fast as the speed
of sound.

       ***

Chapters of the Torah repeat over
the flow of our lives: Esav again
plots against his brother, itching
his bronze beard in the noon light,
flexing his longbow,
muscles hard as any pillar;
nimble women, heavy wine,
blood-roasted meat
also on his mind.

       ***

Elementary school felt like wearing granite shoes
in the murky Lehigh River:

The screams of the rabbi ripped me
from the dreams of girls
whose forms had just begun
to emerge from dark waters.

I was forced back
to Deuteronomy,
the end of it all,

the path back
to the start.

    ***

Moses dies on top of Mt. Nebo,
high above the land of Moab,
with great longing
to reach the holy land.

Next year, he will be born
once more— his home drowned
in the light of his soul.

He will bite the red-hot coal,
lead the slaves impossibly through
the Sea of Reeds—
not straight, but in a horseshoe
pattern, curved like time.

    ***

Time can be warped by gravity—
moments losing all definition

A black hole's density and pull
distorts the movement
of time in ways
we have no means
of tracing.

    ***

Time teases us:
the days she spent with me
always seem recent—
were years ago.

I still see the shadows
of long oak branches
cast by dry lightning
as we raced to her
home in Jersey City.

She's always revving
her silver convertible,
roof down, racing
away from me.

      ***

No one can say ages
were not contracted
by the pull of a black hole
and squeezed into the time prior
to Adam devouring the fruit
of knowledge—
filling the world
with confusion.

Time is also a coil,
repeating lessons.
Here, man sees
he cannot leave
his wife—even
after the shared
flavor of sin.

      ***

The twelve spies are dispatched
to Canaan again this year.
Fear rumbles their spines; they tell
their lies, not for fear
of the Canaanites—
but the dread of life

without falling manna,
protection
from the venom
of snakes,
of scorpions,
of tedious work.

Sowing the fields is the way
it must be: we live as flesh
and spark, part eternal,
part finite, as scholars
and hard-working grape
pressers splashed with mud,
like the great Rashi.

   ***

Time stood still so Joshua could stamp out
the 5-nation army— from Goshen to Givon—
before darkness dropped.

G-d threw down fiery rocks
on the Jews' enemies that day,
and they were no more.

Time stood still once more
in the haze of a cab
as I stared at another woman
arguing with myself over what to do,
the traffic lights of Time Square
spilling red light between us.

I should have touched
her pale hand, leaned
into the gleaming
of her large lips—

which Esav would have
claimed on first sight, taking her
to a cold cave above
the hunting grounds
and fields of trembling wheat.

    ***

In 9th grade, I decide to be
a student one day. From then on,
I am a student.

Time speeds up when
I learn radiant words
elevating from the page:

The candle of G-d
is the soul of man.

Time curves back to 1798—
the Alter Rebbe elucidating
those words from Proverbs:

A soul, like a flame,
wishes to be swallowed
in its source above.

    ***

All we have are metaphors
for the Divine like children
have stuffed animals
they someday forget.

G-d can see from the start
until the end— framed
in a single scene.

One day, this world
must return to the start
or flash out.

The Loudest Language

The broken heart is the master key,
said the Baal Shem Tov.

Despair is the loudest language
in all worlds.

Ask the mother of the stolen seven-year-old girl.
Ask the widowed wives still in love.
Ask the newly dead as they look down.
Ask the soldier missing both arms.

The broken heart is the master key,
said the Chassidic master
to the shofar blower who lost
his page of mystical notations
& thought he had failed his task—

having blasted notes
like a simple,
broken man.

Acknowledgments and Profound Thanks:

My mom and dad, my siblings— especially Yehoshua November— and their families, along with Jared Harel, Joey Nicoletti, Julia Knobloch, Larry Yudelson, Rabbi Shlomo Kugel, Rodger Kamanetz, Alan Shapiro, Phil Terman, Maria Mazziotti Gillan, Alicia Ostriker the emissaries of Chabad, and all my colleagues at Touro University.

Special thanks to Karla Cohen, the amazing and generous artist who created the art for the cover. You can find her work at karlacohenart.com.

Special thanks to Bill Lewis, a wonderful boss.

In memory of Shirin Ilkhan.

"After Esav" was featured in *Poetica Magazine*.

"After Bracha," "Victor 'Young' Perez," "Self-Portrait with the Baal Shem Tov," "For a Few Holy Sparks," and "A Gift in the Shallows of the Sea" were featured in *Vox Populi*.

"City of No Tulips" was featured in WONDERLUST.

"Tourists in Love" was featured in *Tiferet Journal*.

"Dance Lessons for Jews," "An Education," "An Event for Jewish Singles," and "The Pop-Up Rave of Jerusalem" were featured in *The Lehrhaus*.

"Throughout the 7th Night" was featured in the *Jewish Literary Journal*.

"The Stars Drowned Beneath Us," "The Stocked Spring," and "The End is the Beginning is the End" were or will be featured in *Paterson Literary Review*.

"You are Witness" and "To be Wicks" were featured in *The Nu Review*.

"Closer to Mars" was featured in *The Main Street Rag*.

"The Talmud's Fool," "The Tethered Life," "Bitter Departures," and "The Destruction of Our Temple" were featured in *Judith Magazine*.

About the Author

Baruch November's prominent works include the Pushcart Prize-nominated poem "After Esav;" *Bar Mitzvah Dreams*, a book which Stephen Dobyns praised as "one of the best he had recently read;" and *Dry Nectars of Plenty*, winner of BigCityLit's chapbook contest. Thomas Lux has called November "a poet of talent, urgency, and a large and aching heart." November's works have also been featured in *The American Scholar, Lumina, Paterson Literary Review, Tiferet Journal, NewMyths.com*, and the *Forward*. He serves as co-host of the Jewish Poetry Reading Series, which has featured Linda Pastan, Grace Schulman, and others. For two decades, Baruch November has taught Shakespeare, Multicultural American Literature, Poetry, Fiction, and Creative Writing at Touro University in Manhattan. He has lived in many cities across the United States, but currently resides in Washington Heights, New York.

The Jewish Poetry Project

jpoetry.us

Ben Yehuda Press

From the Coffee House of Jewish Dreamers: Poems of Wonder and Wandering and the Weekly Torah Portion by Isidore Century

"Isidore Century is a wonderful poet. His poems are funny, deeply observed, without pretension." — *The Jewish Week*

The House at the Center of the World: Poetic Midrash on Sacred Space by Abe Mezrich

"Direct and accessible, Mezrich's midrashic poems often tease profound meaning out of his chosen Torah texts. These poems remind us that our Creator is forgiving, that the spiritual and physical can inform one another, and that the supernatural can be carried into the everyday."
—Yehoshua November, author of *God's Optimism*

we who desire: Poems and Torah riffs by Sue Swartz

"Sue Swartz does magnificent acrobatics with the Torah. She takes the English that's become staid and boring, and adds something that's new and strange and exciting. These are poems that leave a taste in your mouth, and you walk away from them thinking, what did I just read? Oh, yeah. It's the Bible."
—Matthue Roth, author of *Yom Kippur A Go-Go*

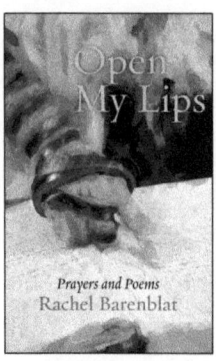

Open My Lips: Prayers and Poems by Rachel Barenblat

"Barenblat's God is a personal God—one who lets her cry on His shoulder, and who rocks her like a colicky baby. These poems bridge the gap between the ineffable and the human. This collection will bring comfort to those with a religion of their own, as well as those seeking a relationship with some kind of higher power."
—Satya Robyn, author of *The Most Beautiful Thing*

Words for Blessing the World: Poems in Hebrew and English by Herbert J. Levine

"These writings express a profoundly earth-based theology in a language that is clear and comprehensible. These are works to study and learn from."
—Rodger Kamenetz, author of *The Jew in the Lotus*

Shiva Moon: Poems by Maxine Silverman

"The poems, deeply felt, are spare, spoken in a quiet but compelling voice, as if we were listening in to her inner life. This book is a precious record of the transformation saying Kaddish can bring."
—Howard Schwartz, author of *The Library of Dreams*

is: heretical Jewish blessings and poems by Yaakov Moshe (Jay Michaelson)

"Finally, Torah that speaks to and through the lives we are actually living: expanding the tent of holiness to embrace what has been cast out, elevating what has been kept down, advancing what has been held back, reveling in questions, revealing contradictions."
—Eden Pearlstein, aka eprhyme

Texts to the Holy: Poems
by Rachel Barenblat

"These poems are remarkable, radiating a love of God that is full bodied, innocent, raw, pulsating, hot, drunk. I can hardly fathom their faith but am grateful for the vistas they open. I will sit with them, and invite you to do the same."
—Merle Feld, author of *A Spiritual Life*

The Sabbath Bee: Love Songs to Shabbat
by Wilhelmina Gottschalk

"Torah, say our sages, has seventy faces. As these prose poems reveal, so too does Shabbat. Here we meet Shabbat as familiar housemate, as the child whose presence transforms a family, as a spreading tree, as an annoying friend who insists on being celebrated, as a woman, as a man, as a bee, as the ocean."
—Rachel Barenblat, author of *The Velveteen Rabbi's Haggadah*

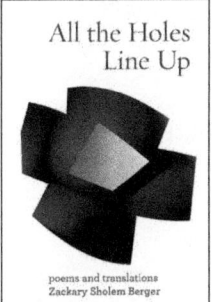

All the Holes Line Up: Poems and Translations
by Zackary Sholem Berger

"Spare and precise, Berger's poems gaze unflinchingly at—but also celebrate—human imperfection in its many forms. And what a delight that Berger also includes in this collection a handful of his resonant translations of some of the great Yiddish poets." —Yehoshua November, author of *God's Optimism* and *Two World Exist*

How to Bless the New Moon:
Songs of the Sovereign and the Icon
by Rachel Kann

"Rachel Kann is a master wordsmith. Her poems are rich in content, packed with life's wisdom and imbued with soul. May this collection of her work enable more of the world to enjoy her offerings."
—Sarah Yehudit Schneider, author of *You Are What You Hate* and *Kabbalistic Writings on the Nature of Masculine and Feminine*

Into My Garden
by David Caplan

"The beauty of Caplan's book is that it is not polemical. It does not set out to win an argument or ask you whether you've put your tefillin on today. These gentle poems invite the reader into one person's profound, ambiguous religious experience."
—*The Jewish Review of Books*

Between the Mountain and the Land is the Lesson: Poetic Midrash on Sacred Community
by Abe Mezrich

"Abe Mezrich cuts straight back to the roots of the Midrashic tradition, sermonizing as a poet, rather than idealogue. Best of all, Abe knows how to ask questions and avoid the obvious answers."
—Jake Marmer, author of *Jazz Talmud*

NOKADDISH: Poems in the Void
by Hanoch Guy Kaner

"A subversive, midrashic play with meanings—specifically Jewish meanings, and then the reversal and negation of these meanings."
—Robert G. Margolis

An Added Soul: Poems for a New Old Religion
by Herbert J. Levine

"Herbert J. Levine's lovely poems swing wide the double doors of English and Hebrew and open on the awe of being. Clear and direct, at ease in both tongues, these lyrics embrace a holiness unyoked from myth and theistic searching."
—Lynn Levin, author, *The Minor Virtues*

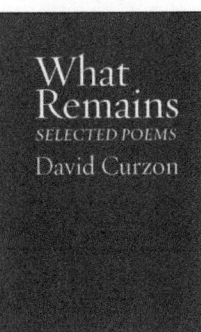

What Remains
by David Curzon

"Aphoristic, ekphrastic, and precise revelations animate WHAT REMAINS. In his stunning rewriting of Psalm 1 and other biblical passages, Curzon shows himself to be a fabricator, a collector, and an heir to the literature, arts, and wisdom traditions of the planet."
—Alicia Ostriker, author of *The Volcano and After*

The Shortest Skirt in Shul
by Sass Oron

"These poems exuberantly explore gender, Torah, the masks we wear, and the way our bodies (and the ways we wear them) at once threaten stable narratives, and offer the kind of liberation that saves our lives."
—Alicia Jo Rabins, author of *Divinity School*, composer of *Girls In Trouble*

Walking Triptychs
by Ilya Gutner

These are poems from when I walked about Shanghai and thought about the meaning of the Holocaust.

Book of Failed Salvation
by Julia Knobloch

"These beautiful poems express a tender longing for spiritual, physical, and emotional connection. They detail a life in movement—across distances, faith, love, and doubt."
—David Caplan, author of *Into My Garden*

Daily Blessings: Poems on Tractate Berakhot
by Hillel Broder

"Hillel Broder does not just write poetry about the Talmud; he also draws out the Talmud's poetry, finding lyricism amidst legality and re-setting the Talmud's rich images like precious gems in end-stopped lines of verse."
—Ilana Kurshan, author of *If All the Seas Were Ink*

The Missing Jew: Poems 1976-2022
by Rodger Kamenetz

"How does Rodger Kamenetz manage to have so singular a voice and at the same time precisely encapsulate the world view of an entire generation (also mine) of text-hungry American Jews born in the middle of the twentieth century?"
—Jacqueline Osherow, author of *Ultimatum from Paradise* and *My Lookalike at the Krishna Temple: Poems*

The Red Door: A dark fairy tale told in poems
by Shawn C. Harris

"The Red Door, like its poet author Shawn C. Harris, transcends genres and identities. It is an exploration in crossing worlds. It brings together poetry and story telling, imagery and life events, spirit and body, the real and the fantastic, Jewish past and Jewish present, to spin one tale."
—Einat Wilf, author of *The War of Return*

The Matter of Families
by Robert H. Deluty

"Robert Deluty's career-spanning collection of New and Selected poems captures the essence of his work: the power of love, joy, and connection, all tied together with the poet's glorious sense of humor. This book is Deluty's masterpiece."
—Richard M. Berlin, M.D., author of *Freud on My Couch*

The Five Books of Limericks
by Rhonda Rosenheck

"A biblical commentary that is truly unique. Each chapter of the Torah is distilled into its own limerick, leading the reader to reconsider the meaning of the original text, and opening avenues for interpretation that are both fun and insightful."
—Rabbi Hillel Norry

Bits and Pieces
by Edward Pomerantz

"A stunning tapestry of family life in the 40s and 50s. Like all great poetry, Pomerantz's work expands after reading. Each poem is exquisitely structured, often with a stunning ending, into a masterful whole."
—Alan Ziegler, editor of SHORT: An International Anthology

Words for a Dazzling Firmament: Poems/Readings on Bereishit Through Shemot
by Abe Mezrich

"Mezrich is a cultivated craftsman— interpretively astute, sonically deliberate, and spiritually cunning."
—Zohar Atkins, author of Nineveh

Everything Thaws
by R. B. Lemberg

"Full of glacier-sharp truths, and moments revealed between words like bodies beneath melting permafrost. As it becomes increasingly plain how deeply our world is shaped by war and climate change and grief and anger, articulating that shape feels urgent and necessary and painful and healing."
—Ruthanna Emrys, author of A Half-Built Garden

Ode to the Dove
An illustrated, bilingual edition of a Yiddish poem by Abraham Sutzkever
Zackary Sholem Berger, translator
Liora Ostroff, Illustrator

"An elegant volume for lovers of poetry."
—Justin Cammy, translator of *Sutzkever, From the Vilna Ghetto to Nuremberg: Memoir and Testimony*

Poems for a Cartoon Mouse
by Andrew Burt

"Andrew Burt's poetry magnifies the vanishingly small line between danger and safety. This collection asks whether order is an illusion that veils chaos, or vice-versa, juxtaposing images from the Bible with animated films."
—Ari Shapiro, host of NPR's *All Things Considered*

Old Shul
by Pinny Bulman

"Nostalgia gives way to a tender theology, a softly chuckling illumination from within the heart of/as a beautiful, broken sanctuary, somehow both gritty and fragile, grimy and iridescent – not unlike faith itself."
—Jake Marmer, author of *Cosmic Diaspora*

Feet In L.A., But My Womb Lives In Jerusalem, My Breath In Vermont
by Lori Levy

"Reading through Lori Levy's new book of poems takes my breath away. With no pretense whatsoever, they leap, alive, from the page until this reader felt as if she were living Levy's life. How does the author do it?"
—Mary Jo Balistreri, author of *Still*

www.ingramcontent.com/pod-product-compliance
Lightning Source LLC
LaVergne TN
LVHW041343080426
835512LV00006B/594